For my sweet, talented daughter, Aimee,
writer, photographer, filmmaker—Awesome! —J.B.G.

To the little dreamers
who are fascinated by the wonders of Earth. —T.G.

Clarion Books is an imprint of HarperCollins Publishers.

Awesome Earth
Text copyright © 2025 by Joan Bransfield Graham
Art copyright © 2025 by Tania Garcia
Photographs copyright © 2025 by Joan Bransfield Graham

Library of Congress Cataloging-in-Publication Data

Names: Graham, Joan Bransfield, author. | Garcia, Tania, illustrator.
Title: Awesome Earth / by Joan Bransfield Graham ; illustrated by Tania Garcia .
Description: First edition. | New York, NY : Clarion Books, an imprint of HarperCollins Publishers, [2025] | Audience: Ages 4–8.
| Audience: Grades Preschool–3. | Summary: Concrete poems illustrate how our Earth slowly took shape.
Identifiers: LCCN 2022058382 | ISBN 9780358396048 (hardcover)
Subjects: LCSH: Earth (Planet)—Juvenile poetry. | Children's poetry, American. | Concrete poetry, American. | CYAC: Earth
(Planet)—Poetry. | Concrete poetry. | American poetry. | LCGFT: Concrete poetry. | Picture books.
Classification: LCC PS3557.R213 Aw 2024 | DDC 811/.54—dc23/eng/20230517
LC record available at https://lccn.loc.gov/2022058382

The artist used digital techniques combined with handmade ink textures created from sponges, scourers,
old brushes, wrinkled plastics, and old eyelash mascaras to create the digital illustrations for this book.
Typography by Cara Llewellyn and Caitlin E. D. Stamper
24 25 26 27 28   RTLO   10 9 8 7 6 5 4 3 2 1

First Edition

AWESOME EARTH

CONCRETE POEMS
CELEBRATE CAVES, CANYONS,
AND OTHER FASCINATING LANDFORMS

JOAN BRANSFIELD GRAHAM
ILLUSTRATED BY TANIA GARCÍA

CLARION BOOKS
An Imprint of HarperCollinsPublishers

FANTASTIC FORCES

The Earth is
unsettled, it would seem,
for here and about it lets off
steam. Lava flows, geysers gush,
canyons are carved by a river's push.
The Earth's old crust cracks and creaks,
shakes and shoves up mountain peaks.
Ice caps recede, glaciers advance,
ever in motion—a global dance.
Will it ever stand still?
Not a chance!

CONTINENTS

puzzle pieces—
the continental
drift never ceases.
Seven continents,
and it's still
not done.
But remember
it once was
only ONE.

At one
start, the Earth
pulled apart, separated—a
division quite monumental,
when things b e c a m e
c o n t i n e n t a l.
Landmasses
shaped
L
I
K
E

MOUNTAIN

Up,
Up, Up,
peak upon
peak, I seek
the sky. Enrobed
with snow, still high,
higher I go—far past the
horizon. My view of the world is
vast. I pierce the clouds. Come climb
with me, see what I see—I AM MOUNTAIN!

DESERT

Shape-shifter,
dune-drifter, sand-sifter,
hot desert winds build billowy dunes,
an ever-changing ocean of sand, an arid land.

Camels
don't retreat,
their bodies survive the
scorching heat. Cover your
faces in these wind-whipped places.

VOLCANO

Once I begin to
blow my top, I
just can't STOP!
B E W A R E !
Don't breathe
my s m o k y air!
Bubbling, churning,
burning HOT, with all
the power that I've got,
molten M A G M A, lava,
starts to F L O W —
WATCH OUT, WATCH OUT,
WATCH OUT BELOW !!!

L
A
V
A

L
A
V
A

CHASM

A crease,
slash
in the
Earth,
a slip,
dive,
dip—
what
ripped
the
land?

Was
it a
tectonic,
seismic
spasm
that
caused
this
steep-
sided
chasm?

Or the

constant

shiver of

a fast-flowing

river?

ROCK IT!

IGNEOUS

Magma, lava,
molten fire all
conspire . . . go with
the F L O W in a
messy spill, and then
they COOL IT, C H I L L,
take stock—discover
they've turned into
IGNEOUS ROCK!

SEDIMENTARY

Stacked up,
layer after layer,
SEDIMENTARY ROCK
is an important player.
Erosion won't let
all of it last, but its
strata has data from
ages past.

METAMORPHIC

METAMORPHIC ROCK
morphs, changes,
transforms, rearranges—
pressure and heat
make the switch
complete.

CAVE

W H A T treasures does this deep cave hold—
silver, diamonds, gleaming gold?
Bones that make you shiver, quiver—
a hidden river? Or maybe on the
ceiling, the starlike effervescence
of glowworms' bioluminescence.

STALACTITES

Slowly, slowly, through the ground, water drips, slips

d
o
w
n,

evaporates, leaves art behind, a f i n e mineral-inspired

d
e
s
i
g
n.

STALAGMITES

W
h
i
l
e
on
the
cave
floor,
droplets
G R O W,

c
a
l
c
i
f
y,
put on
a mighty
show. How
H I G H can
they G O???

ARCHES

Artistry of the Earth, our sandstone sculpted by water and time into shapes sublime.

We sweep across the sky, catch your eye, defy gravity.

No two the same . . . we are both *art* and *frame*.

ISLAND

Water, water, everywhere—
waves lap, leap, encircle me in a river,
lake, ocean, or sea. I might be a continental island,
if you get my drift, or an oceanic island due to lava's lift. If I'm
small, I can be an islet, motu, or key—that's a mini-me. Come visit
by plane, bridge, or set sail, discovering dolphins and, maybe—a whale.

ARCHIPELAGO

A chain,
a ribbon,

a story of
islands

like
stars

in a

constellation.

PENINSULA

Jutting out into the sea, here I stand—
but still anchored, connected to the land.
Water on three sides,
"almost an island"—
but not quite.
What size?
I might be
large or small.
I'm afraid that
I must boast.
I've got miles
a n d   m i l e s
of r o c k y
or s a n d y,
d a n d y
coast!

GLACIER

A
mountain,
a river of ice,
I do not race. I
move at a glacial pace,
inching, grinding, picking up
pebbles, rocks along the way.
I do not stay still, I chisel forward,
sometimes leaving in my wake . . .

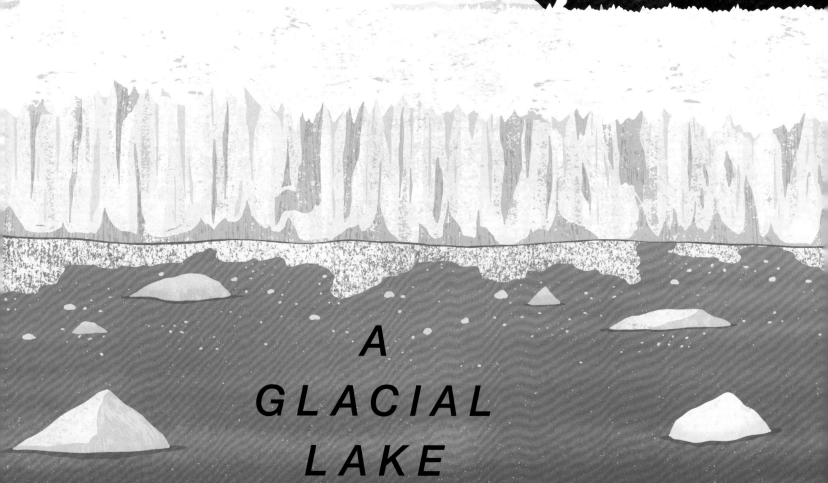

*A
GLACIAL
LAKE*

PLAIN

HOW DO YOU EXPLAIN THIS TYPE OF TERRAIN?
ACRES OF FOREVER THAT NEVER SEEM TO END,
RIPPLING G R A I N . . . WAVES OF W H E A T—
A GRASSLAND, PRAIRIE, SAVANNA, TUNDRA,
DEPENDING ON THE FREEZING COLD OR HEAT.
A PLAIN CAN R E S T BESIDE A RIVER OR
LOUNGE BY THE SEA—SUCH VERSATILITY!

PLATEAU

A high plain, did you know,
is tableland or a . . . p l a t e a u.
Level, flat, lifted by geologic forces,
shaped by rivers, wind, rain—many sources—
worn down in certain places, creating canyons, buttes, or mesas.
A form fated to be ELEVATED.

Somewhere there's
a river that will
deliver an
erosion explosion,
not quickly, but over
millions of years—

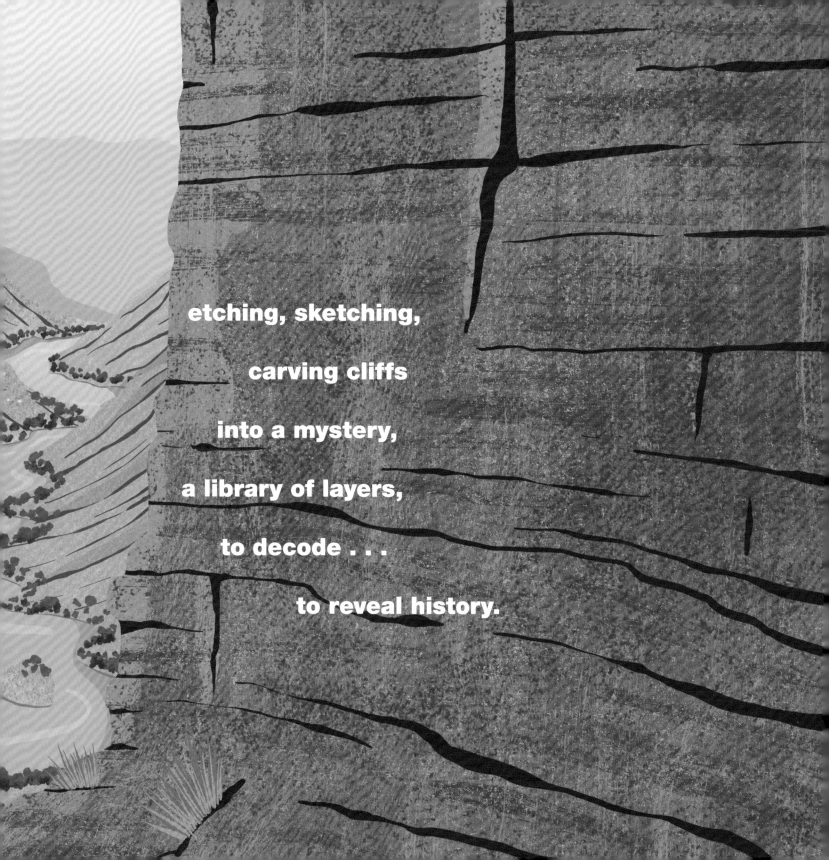

etching, sketching,

carving cliffs

into a mystery,

a library of layers,

to decode . . .

to reveal history.

HILLS

Mounds,
rounded, rippling ribs
roll, spill across the horizon—

fill,
enchant the
skies, delight,

surprise
your eyes with
spring splendor . . . a
brilliant scene of new green.

VALLEYS

Hills
and mountains
are the UP, while

with
a regal, living
emerald crown.

VALLEYS are the DOWN,
below, on the ground,
rimmed all around

HOODOOS

HOODOOS
SO
MANY
HUES
OF RED
ORANGE
TAN

YOU
SCATTER
LIGHT—
A
STRIKING
SIGHT

BOLDLY
YOU
STAND
PAINTING
SHADOWS
ON
THE
LAND

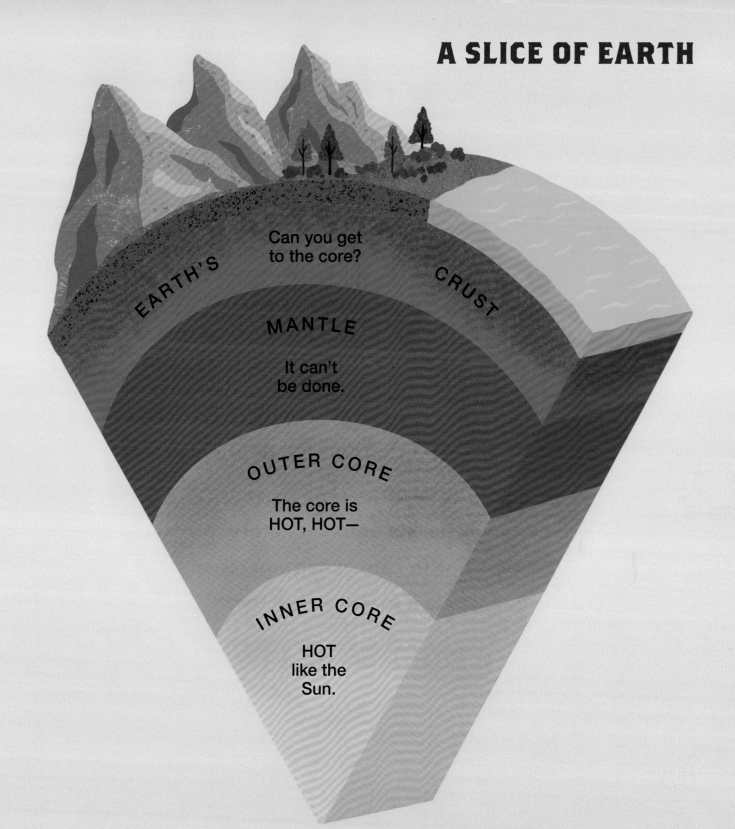

A SLICE OF EARTH

Can you get to the core?

EARTH'S

CRUST

MANTLE

It can't be done.

OUTER CORE

The core is HOT, HOT—

INNER CORE

HOT like the Sun.

ARTIST

The Earth is
an artist, at work every
day, with powerful tools that
come into play: pressure, time, wind,
water, ice, too—all forming wondrous
features to view. It sculpts, chisels, carves,
etches, creating awe-inspiring sketches.
Explore the world, enjoy its glory, listen
to it whisper its unfolding story. Walk
gently, with care, when you roam.
Earth is a treasure, the Earth
is our home.

CONTINENTS

During Earth's 4.5-billion-year history, gigantic landmasses, or supercontinents, formed, broke apart, and drifted across the surface of the Earth to create the seven **continents** we have today. When you look at a map, the continents seem like puzzle pieces that could fit together—especially South America and Africa! Scientists found that the Earth's crust is divided into huge slabs of rock called **tectonic plates**. When these plates move toward, away from, or past each other, they can cause **continental drift**, as well as create volcanoes, earthquakes, and mountains.

MOUNTAIN

A **mountain** can be formed by colliding tectonic plates, and some continue to grow a small amount each year. Around 40–50 million years ago, after India broke off from Madagascar, it crashed into Asia, pushing up the Himalayan Mountain range, which includes Mount Everest, the world's tallest mountain above sea level.

DESERT

Wind, climate patterns, and lack of rain contribute to the formation of a **desert**. An **oasis** is a small area in a desert where water comes up to the surface and plants grow. Instead of water, a camel's hump stores up to eighty pounds (thirty-six kilograms) of fat, which helps it survive for months without food. Bushy eyebrows, double rows of long eyelashes, a clear inner "eyelid," and nostrils that close all protect camels in sandstorms. The largest (nonpolar) desert is the Sahara in Africa.

VOLCANO

A **volcano** can take shape when one tectonic plate sinks beneath another or where plates spread apart and magma oozes up. **Magma** is hot, molten rock stored deep within the Earth. **Lava** is magma that has risen to the Earth's surface through a volcano. Many of the Earth's volcanoes are located around the Pacific Ocean in a region called the Ring of Fire. One of the world's most active volcanoes is Mount Kīlauea (*kill-uh-WAY-uh*); its lava has added hundreds of acres of new land to Hawaii's Big Island.

CHASM

Cracks in the Earth's crust, or geological faults, can cause a **chasm**, which might then be scoured by receding glaciers and eroded by rapid river water. The Ausable River that flows to Lake Champlain helped shape New York's Ausable Chasm, which features sheer sandstone walls 500 million years old.

ROCK IT! (IGNEOUS, SEDIMENTARY, METAMORPHIC)

There are three main types of rocks. **Igneous** rocks, from the Latin for *fire*, form from magma or lava. **Sedimentary** rocks contain layers of rock fragments, remains of microscopic organisms, and minerals that can provide clues to help us learn what life was like millions of years ago and whether the land was once beneath an ocean. Heat and pressure deep within the Earth form **metamorphic** rocks, such as marble and slate.

CAVE

Most **caves**, hollows in the ground, develop when water mixes with soluble rock, often limestone, and dissolves it, eroding it from within. Rivers, waves, lava, earthquakes, glaciers, and wind can also cause caves. **Bioluminescence** is a chemical reaction in the body of a living creature that allows it to give off its own light. In Waitomo, New Zealand, glowworms on the ceilings of caves look like hundreds of stars. Once underwater, this limestone formation developed into caves over 30 million years.

STALACTITES / STALAGMITES

When water drips through limestone in caves, it dissolves minerals, then evaporates to **calcify**, leaving behind hardened deposits of calcium carbonate. This action can create icicle-like **stalactites** (think *c* as in "hanging from the *ceiling*") and **stalagmites** (think *g* as in "rising from the *ground*"). If a stalactite and stalagmite join together, they form a column. All of these features appear in Guilin, China, in the Reed Flute Cave, which is over 180 million years old.

ARCHES

Sedimentary rock called **sandstone** is made up of compressed grains of sand and quartz. It is usually red, yellow, or brown. The over two thousand natural stone **arches** in Arches National Park in Utah evolved in a process that took about 65 million years. Today, water seeping into cracks, freezing, and expanding continues to sculpt the rock into its dramatic shapes.

(Left) Bora Bora, with two motus, small islands, part of Society Islands **archipelago** in the South Pacific.

(Right) Zion National Park, Utah, includes this example of **sedimentary rock**—"Court of the Patriarchs," named for biblical figures Abraham, Isaac, and Jacob.

ISLAND

A **continental island** is surrounded by water but close to a continent. **Oceanic islands** rise to the surface from the seafloor and are formed by volcanic action. Greenland, the world's largest island, is a continental island on the North American Plate.

ARCHIPELAGO

An **archipelago** (ark-ih-PELL-ih-go) is a group of islands, such as the strings of islands that make up Japan, Hawaii, and Indonesia. A great number of archipelagos were created by volcanoes and are located near hot spots, which are plumes of magma rising from deep within the Earth.

PENINSULA

A **peninsula** is often caused by rising and falling sea levels. The state of Florida is mostly a peninsula, with the Atlantic Ocean on its east coast and the Gulf of Mexico to its west. The largest peninsula in the world is the Arabian Peninsula.

GLACIER

A **glacier** is a moving body of ice that travels by its own weight and gravity. Over millions of years, it can sculpt mountains, move huge quantities of soil and rocks, and carve valleys and lakes. Glaciers store the largest supply of fresh water on Earth and help keep our planet cool by reflecting the sun's rays. Rapid glacial melt is causing sea levels to rise. Lambert Glacier in Antarctica is the world's largest.

PLAIN

Sediment deposited by water, ice, wind, and erosion, as well as lava flow, can form **plains.** Wide, mostly flat grasslands, plains make up over one-third of the Earth's surface. They include **prairies**, with moderate temperatures and few trees, **tundras**, which are treeless with frozen ground, and **savannas**, tropical areas with small, scattered trees, like Africa's Serengeti Plain, a home to many varieties of wildlife.

PLATEAU

When magma presses upward but is unable to break through Earth's surface, it can push up an area of the crust to create a **plateau.** Tectonic plates colliding to lift land, layering of lava over time, and erosion can also form plateaus. The Tibetan Plateau is the highest, largest plateau in the world and an important water source for Asia.

CANYON

What stories the exposed walls of canyons hold! Carved from the Colorado Plateau by erosion and the Colorado River over 5–6 million years, Arizona's Grand Canyon shows layers of rocks and minerals that span about 1.5 billion years, around one-third of the Earth's life. The Grand Canyon is bigger than the state of Rhode Island.

HILLS

Glaciers, water currents, wind, rain, faults, and erosion all can form **hills**—raised land with sloping sides. While hills often display many shades of green, on Bohol Island in the Philippines, there are over 1,268 cone-shaped Chocolate Hills, which turn brown and look like giant chocolate drops during the dry season.

VALLEYS

Valleys, the lowland areas between hills or mountains, can be carved by rivers or streams (if V-shaped) or glaciers (when U-shaped) or formed by the movement of the Earth's crust. In California's Antelope Valley, if a cold winter cracks open their seeds, enough rain falls to help them grow, and high winds don't harm them, a superbloom of poppies paints the hills and valleys orange-gold.

HOODOOS

Hoodoos are tall spires of rock weathered and eroded by rain, ice, and wind. Minerals within the different rocks give hoodoos varying colors. Bryce Canyon in Utah, a series of natural amphitheaters, features the greatest concentration of hoodoos on Earth.

A SLICE OF EARTH

Earth's **crust** is a thin, rigid outermost layer of igneous, sedimentary, and metamorphic rocks and minerals. Beneath the crust is the **mantle**, molten rock that can mold and stretch without breaking. It is always moving, but very slowly. The dense center of the Earth is larger than the planet Mars. It consists of the **outer core** of *liquid* iron and nickel, which spins as the planet rotates, creating the Earth's magnetic field, and the **inner core**, which is *solid* iron and nickel due to immense pressure.

GLOSSARY

CONSTELLATION—A group of stars that form a pattern, which is given a name inspired by its shape. The Big Dipper is part of the constellation Ursa Major, the Great Bear.

CONTINENT—One of the major landmasses of the globe. The seven continents, from largest to smallest, are Asia, Africa, North America, South America, Antarctica, Europe, and Australia.

CONTINENTAL DRIFT—The theory that over millions of years the continents have moved, or drifted, over the surface of the Earth

EARTHQUAKE—A sudden rolling or shaking of the Earth, caused when rock breaks along a fault or when tectonic plates grind past each other, sending seismic waves through the ground

EROSION—A geological process where natural forces such as water, ice, wind, and gravity move soil and rock, wearing down the surface of the Earth

EVAPORATE—To change from a liquid or solid into vapor (like mist, fog, or steam); to disappear

GEOLOGY—The science that studies the story of the Earth—its history told by its rocks, landforms, and physical structures, and how they are created and changed over time

GRAVITY—The force by which a planet, or other body, draws objects toward its center

LANDFORMS—Natural physical features of the Earth's surface that are defined by shape, location, and how they developed

LIMESTONE—A sedimentary rock usually formed at the bottom of a lake or sea from sand, mud, fossil fragments, and shells, which have been compressed over time

MAGNETIC FIELD—The Earth acts like a giant magnet. Its magnetic field, an invisible zone of force around it, shields and protects us by deflecting, or pushing away, harmful rays from the sun.

MINERALS—Formed naturally, minerals are solid, inorganic (nonliving), and have a distinct crystal structure. Quartz, gold, silver, and copper are all minerals.

SEISMIC—Relating to earthquakes or other vibrations of the Earth and its crust

STRATA (or **STRATUM**, singular noun)—Unique layers of rock or soil in sedimentary rock, often from different periods of time

SUPERBLOOM—Typically, every ten years or so in the spring in California, an explosion of poppies and wildflowers will burst into bloom at the same time, carpeting the deserts with dazzling colors.

SUPERCONTINENT—A very large landmass that contains or connects most or all of the land on Earth

TECTONIC PLATE THEORY—A theory in geology that says that the Earth's crust is divided into huge slabs of rock, which float over the molten mantle beneath. When these tectonic plates move toward, away from, or grind past each other, they can create mountains, volcanoes, and earthquakes.

TERRAIN—The physical features or topography of a stretch of land or geographic area

WEATHERING—The breaking down, loosening, or wearing away of a substance so that forces of erosion, such as wind, ice, and rain, can carry parts of it away

ADDITIONAL RESOURCES TO EXPLORE

American Museum of Natural History—Read about important discoveries in geology by Inge Lehmann, Harry Hess, James Hutton, and more.
amnh.org/learn-teach/curriculum-collections/earth-inside-and-out
amnh.org/explore/ology/earth

National Aeronautics and Space Administration (NASA)—Earth observations from space can help solve challenges here on our planet.
nasa.gov/topics/earth/index.html
nasa.gov/SpaceforUS

National Geographic—Learn more about continental drift and landforms.
nationalgeographic.org/encyclopedia/continental-drift
nationalgeographic.org/encyclopedia/landform

(Above Left) A "Brilliant" **stalagmite** in Postojna **Cave**, Slovenia, is 16.4 feet (5 meters) tall.

(Above Right) Vernal Falls at Yosemite National Park, California, where much of the rock is granite, a type of **igneous rock**.

(Above) In the Reed Flute **Cave**, Guilin, China, colored lights illuminate **stalactites** in "Nature's Art Palace."

(Left) The California Poppy Reserve in Antelope Valley, California, a high desert **plateau** grassland of the Mojave Desert, displays a superbloom of poppies and wildflowers.

National Park Service (NPS)—As their website says, "explore the world's most magnificent rock collection—your National Parks." Amazing visuals as well as Arts in the Parks, which encourages you to be inspired by the Earth's awesomeness and "find your spark" at a national park.
nps.gov/subjects/geology/index.htm
nps.gov/subjects/arts/index.htm

United States Geological Survey (USGS)—Always available to help and give information during emergencies, especially earthquakes.
usgs.gov/science-support/osqi/yes/resources-teachers
/multimedia-k-2

University of California, Santa Barbara (UCSB)—Have your questions answered by a scientist.
scienceline.ucsb.edu